All in a Pretty Little Row
Dan Provost Chapbooks
2004-2022

ROADSIDE PRESS

Roadside Press
Meredosia, Illinois

foreword

If you are opening this book and have gone as far as reading this fore-word, you probably already know of or at least heard of Dan Provost. I became a member of this club after hearing about this big guy that was at the Beat Poetry Festival in 2008. I was new to the underground poetry community and was only just starting to build up a MySpace network, and didn't get the "memo," therefore, did not attend. As this seemed to be the first gathering where the disparate poets from around the country first got to meet face-to-face, inevitable adventures were had. I was told stories that included borrowed blankets and bruised knuckles that included this big football coach of man with a generous soul and gift of the poesy. I was compelled to look up Dan's words on the innerweb zines, and found poems that struck me hard. I identified with them quite a bit since Dan and I were of a similar age and strug-gled with the incongruities of the sensitive, thinking athlete and the difficulties of trying to define our manhood. His words made me cry.

It wasn't until later that year at Kansas City's First Unregulated Word Festival where I finally met Dan. It was a handshake and an offer to buy me a drink, even though he never heard of me and we just met, a typical example of his friendliness and generosity. During his reading slot, he kept his head down and just recited sentences that cut me over and over. It was then I recognized the kindred mindstream for sure, and thus began a friendship that I must admit was constantly punc-tuated by his beneficence. Striking to my naturally stingy character, his bought drinks, rides from airports, gifted chapbooks, and even an offer to share his hotel room (much to the chagrin of his then girl-friend) in Erie PA during an early Snoetry festival, Dan became my model of magnanimity, an example to follow. I still proudly wear the "Worcester: Paris of the '80s" t-shirt he gave me when he hosted me, John Dorsey, and Alex Nielsen during our Northeast tour. It remains a symbol and reminder for me to keep fighting to be a better person and let the good shine out.

Dan's indominable natural affability and concern for his friends never wavered even as he battled his many internal demons, the demons that are the fodder for his writing. So fair warning, these poems are not the kind that impel one to run out to the backyard and dance with abandon in a Spring shower. They describe a thousand examples of life's unfairness and the ten thousand ways characters in Dan's sphere of existence cope, even if it eventually continues a cycle of misery. He is exceedingly open in these poems about his own sampling of these methods to at least try to defer hurt and their ultimate failure. The merit of this collection is the opportunity for the reader to map the progression of Dan's development from an already fine writer to an extraordinary chronicler of uncomfortable circumstances with detail and nuance, as well as an honesty few can match. With the chronological structure of this book, we also can see his progress through the trial-and-error lessons learned toward, if not a light at the end of a somber tunnel, but a belief there yet may actually be hope, intangible and invisible, at long last.

If the reader is one that enjoys shoves out of their comfort zone like an offensive tackle blocks you onto your ass, versus a trip to a froo-froo fantasyland of love and light and handed-out happiness, this book is for you. Peace of mind must be earned, and Dan Provost's fathomless generosity to experience his disturbing, incredible, and very personal shared journey is your opportunity to work for it.

Steve Goldberg
Author of *History is an Afterthought* (Luchador Press)
Publisher at WhatsInTheBag Press

TOC

My work is always dedicated to my love, Laura & dog, Bella!!!

My thanks to all the editors who published my chapbooks throughout the years. Hopefully, you never stapled your fingers together by mistake.

Thanks also to the many friends I've met in person and online since I've been attempting to write acceptable poetry…

Steve Goldberg, Michael Grover, John Dorsey, J. Lester Allen, John Sweet, Ron D'Alena, Jim Deuchers, Jason Ryberg, Aleathia Drehmer, Rebecca Schumejda, Jason Baldinger, James Duncan, Frank and Erin Readon, Richard Cronberg, Red Focks, Adrian Manning, Lynn Alexander, Marc Bruseke, Glenn Still (RIP), Debbie Kirk, Nathan Graziano, J.D. Nelson, Jason Hardung, Alan Catlin, Mike Zone, John Patrick Robbins, Russell Vidrick, R.M. Engelhardt, Al Winans, Jacklyn Henry, Kevin Ridgeway, Dan Denton, Luis Berriozabel, Wayne Burke, Matthew Sradeja, Dan Crocker, Scott Simmons, Lisa LaTourette (Kid), Scot Young, Mike Taylor (RIP), Misti Rainwater-Lites, Mike & Laura Cleaves and Troy Thomas Schoultz

And all the people I have forgotten to list—Thank you!!!

To my family: Chip & Jane Provost, Judi & Ken Lamarre, Tim & Heather Provost, Debbie Tebau, my nieces, and nephews.

To John Platt and the rest of the Platt family.

Tuesdays & Fridays with Nathan Dittmer.

Last, but certainly least—my extreme gratitude to Michele McDannold, editor of Roadside Press for all the dedicated hours she puts in to publish poetry…

Observing Life While Drinking Rat Milk
Feel Free Press, 2004
James Quinton, Editor

Another Filthy Ride to Work

Worcester, Massachusetts is a strange city.

But I guess all cities are strange in their own way.

Businessmen converse on one corner while
prostitutes are talking shop 50 feet away.

The homeless converge with stockbrokers.

Main Street is a destination for all

The lucky, the money-grubbers, and those who are
scamming death.

Epiphany at Age 41

The sea still parts
ways with the waves
at 6:04 A.M., after an
all-night drinking binge.

Looking to the water for mental comfort.

I still seem to be losing the battle.

Stumbling along the sand during
the early morning hours, avoiding the
joggers, lovers, and well-wishers
who recognize true beauty while
strolling along the Atlantic seaboard.

I see my reflection in the ocean, and as I try not
to fall and drench myself—I realize that I am
A chameleon—a paper clown with too
few desires and too many excuses for escape.

I seek morality—I live murder.

The Fade

She'll take a shot or two with the boys
who still hoot and holler every time
she enters the room.

It helps take away the pain—as she
slowly looks down at her sagging
breast—that once caused men to
drool like rabid dogs.

Her walk once
    stalked
    libido
    on a hot summer day.

Now, time has caught up with her…
And like the decaying statue that no one looks at
                                        anymore,

She often strolls alone.

Accepting a handful of cheers from the
old masturbation crowd.

Her eyes have bags.
Her ass waddles.
The fade has arrived.

These Guys Never Took Sensitivity Class

It is 9 o'clock on a Sunday—not Saturday like the Billy Joel song,
but the hour where the masses realize that freedom of the
unabashed weekend is now dead.

Except for the mischievous few, who maintain the rebel belief that
a streak of Steppenwolf lyrics and a bottle of Jack Daniels will
quench any hatred of the last moments of Sunday.

The laborers, who dread tomorrow, are squeezing a last run at
felonious thoughts at the local tavern. Restless, gargantuan men.
Some who will have to drag their ass out of bed to haul shingles
up skeleton roofs, others who will be pouring concrete at 7 AM in
the 90-degree sun.

Hoisting shot after shot of Whiskey and seizing the remains of a
celebration, that for most, would have ended long ago.

But not these guys, whose chants relay the hatred of their plight.

"My Fuckin Boss—If he tells me to hurry up with them shingles, I'm
gonna kick his ass."

"These beers are going down too good…I see a sick day coming up."

They, (the common man, the working man, the boys) will sadly look
at the clock---each passing second the outlaw persona will have to
fade into a settlement of normalcy.

There are no western shootouts anymore, no more brushing back the
biceps of manhood and sowing of the "wild, wild oats."

However, there will be a few, who will grin the gambler's grin, laying
claim on a chance to provide another day of renegade spirit.

Rolling the dice, taking the drinking train away from Monday and keeping
pace with their brothers.

Hoping that the old stagecoach will hustle into town, taking them far away—to
a place that never refuses to accept their
patronage.

High School Freak

I saw the old high school freak at Dunkin Donuts last Sunday.

He was sitting alone—300 pounds of lard oozing all around the
booth he was trying to get comfortable in.
He was drinking a 24-ounce coffee and devouring a Jelly
doughnut.

Half of which was on his shirt.

As I walked in—ours eyes met.

I recognized him.
He recognized me.

But I quickly looked down, like I was witnessing the last
temptation of Christ.

Hurriedly taking my place in line with the
rest of the accepted.

He looked down and studied his coffee, a living testament to
the dead soul of the maladjusted crowd.

Improper Balance

Sometimes my identity is a cross between a Norse legend and a
Bukowski bender.

Conquering divine spirit with a scream towards heaven, then showing
a sheepish grin while walking like an animal towards the steps of
hell.

I love being on the border between rock hard erections and soft
filling grocery shoppers who plan their week around buying lettuce
and frozen pizza.

I am worshipped by the Chamber of Commerce—hated by the
whores who fail to get a cent.

Adored by nausea.
Despised by Satan.

Praised by the politicians, cheating on their wives.
Kicked in the nuts by the city's clergy.

Someday, I am hoping that someone will show me how I can avoid the
shadows of splinters, that lay on many of the dirty sidewalks in
any town USA.

Sticks that get lodged in the skin, which serve as a constant
reminder of the battle between filth and gold, outcry and serene.

I hope I am cured soon, because once the fire is extinguished, there's
nothing left but dust and a few rotted bones.

Reading Lifshin

Alone at work, reading Lyn Lifshin's poetry online, gazing out of
my office window wanting the darkness to shield me from
mandatory commonness.

I find studying her stuff to be a simple virtue, juxtaposed in a world of
jargon and misguided pleasure.

But the word can be so exotic…Right, Ms. Lifshin?

While I scan each poem, wondering if someday my tainted talents
will ever be evaluated and discovered?

An uneasy pang of anger shanks me, like the machete used to kill
the adults in Children of the Corn.

Spilling blood on the Lifshin site,
my own selfish blood.

But no, these are not words of death or destruction; poetry can and
should be bare at times.

Each line is a value of some semblance of want.

And her phrases in the Erotic Mirror stun me,
move me, helping to understand the truth that portrays
itself in everyday occasions.

I hope my search will reach its destiny. Finding the way to
filter through what is real and what is just mirror false.

But in the meantime, Lyn Lifshin brings me closer to the answer
without completely falling off the edge.
Without pretense.
Without curtain calls or fanfare.

A Last Run at Youth That Failed

Working on a college campus helps me feel young, even as the
balding flap in the back of my head gets bigger every day.

So, I had to admit, that when I agreed to take out the senior
work-study for a couple of drinks, I was a little excited and aroused.

Her, twenty-one, on the cusp of beginning life in the "real world."
Me—soon to be forty-two, still manning the guns but breaking down
little by
little.

But I had that gleam back, that mid 20-year-old anticipation when
you know
some cocktails will lower inhibitions, and awkward conversation
soon emerges
as laughs of provocative energy.

While the day rolled on, I found myself constantly looking
in the mirror.
Rolling up the sleeves to show the arms.
Tucking in my shirt so the stomach wouldn't protrude.
Picking at my teeth, clipping nose hairs.
Anything to keep that youthful buzz fluttering inside my brain.

Picturing myself sitting at a bar, with a buxom queenie, ready to
get the
party rolling.

When it was time to call it a day—my little charm girl still hadn't
arrived.
I waited…10, 15, 20 minutes, realizing that this dream was a no show.

I let my shirt out, let the sleeves run over my biceps. Put on my Irish
Whiskey hat, and
waited five more minutes.

Hoping she would come over the hill to my office,
Smiling with a sheepish grin.
Giving me the signal
"all systems clear, let's rock and roll."

But that never happened.

Instead, I started my truck and turned the radio to a classic
rock station.

Freebird was blasting through the speakers, and for a minute—I felt like
the mischievous rebel I was during my college days.

I stopped at this little bar, "The French Connection," located in the
dregs of Worcester.
As I ordered a beer, pulling out my money to play some Keno,
I began listening to the conversations some of the patrons
were having.

"Fucking whore, who is she to tell me to stop drinking."
"Ass-hole boss, calls me at six in the morning to finish the addition."
"Are those tits real?"

I looked down at my stomach, the same gut I was trying so hard to hide
all day.

Funny—no one noticed here
          that I was getting
          fat.

Reading About a Drug Deal Gone Bad

For little Jimmy's part in his
daily salary of fifty bucks to
deliver some junk to a guy who
had given up on life long ago.

Jimmy got a bullet to the head.

He's dead.
He's ten.

His bicycle isn't even paid for yet.

One Sunny Wish

A tender game of
puppy love & adolescence chance is being
portrayed for me in the park this morning.

A guy.
A girl.
Each terrified but joyous at the same time.
Hoping their initial shyness will shed its skin in time for serious
interlude and pleasure.

I walk past them.
Three-day growth of beard.
A scowl on my craggy face.

Reeking of Marijuana & lost hope.

And I wonder—whom will I pray for tonight.

Living the Life, Dying the Death

I hope they
find all the
dead poets under
a blanket of loose
change and discarded
condoms.

What a way to go.

2004 Lottery

I saw her face amongst the other migraines that flickered
annoying neon during the lunchtime rush at Sloppy's Pub.

Her fingers were laced with ice picks, as the crowd, who swelled
to a hundred at this point—nonchalantly looked the other way
before the afternoon stabbings.

"This is no Shirley Jackson novel," she said, while purring to the
gambit of men whose bass line pant shuddered the foundation of
the bar.

She licked each nail slowly, threatening to bite each one off at the
nub, then stopping the process and slyly looking over the pitched
tents of the male species that were now oogling her every step.

Each year on the same day this ritual takes place. An unnamed
harlot with power to orgasmisize all men.

Staring through testicular muscle—knifing the drooling patrons
with long, decadent fingers.

As each ejaculated moan became a cry for the stabbing to stop, I
stood in the doorway.

Dumbfounded, alone, insecure.

I then raised my hand and asked her a question.

"What do you have to do to get a drink in here, fuck somebody?"

To the Bum Who Hung out on Salisbury & Killed Himself

In the machine of arrogance, we call the daily hustle and bustle of
the working world, the renegade jumps to his death. Looking for
a final sympathy card in the eyes of apathy.

He was often scavenging, alone on the dregs of a deserted street—
begging for nickels and dimes with the "Help I'm an AIDS Vet,"
sign hung around his neck.

I see him.
I pass him.
You see him.
You pass him.

Never acknowledged or cared about until he bleeds on our
Soft Parade.
He dies quietly on the sidewalk, after a disinterested crowd
shuffles away, hands in pockets—avoiding the body of a
three-story leaper who never took an oath
of commonness.

Small gravestones in small graveyards are filled with many.

Many like him.

Ronnie

The river flowed freely in his backyard.
Music blares at the Juke Joint down the street—The Black Crows
I think.
Here I sit with the judgement of Red Necks embracing my brow.
A working man's existence seen along the water.
We will embrace—and toast Ronnie Van Zant.
Hear the echoes…
Smell the fish that swim along my shore.
Mourn the dead with a tip of the hat,
and a hand on the heart

Real soul has died…

Cold Cut Queen

She'll continue her
                 walk
down Seductive Road &
all
    the
        boys
will be pitching tents because
she'll be
            wearing a low cut
            blouse that will
            reveal bursting cleavage
            that leads neighbors to
            gossip and drool.

And she'll do it again tomorrow.

Wack Off Alley

It's not for the meek that I write these words of beating off under
the canopy of Christian guilt—nor for the sanctity of Jesus Christ,
who
will probably get his old man to beat the shit out of me
while I fantasize
about little Susie Boobie doing my sexual bidding.

No, I was just a horny mortal with the urge to ejaculate razor
blades after striking out at Sloppy's Pub. Never again will I say
the ultimate one liner,

"Hey, do you want to fuck?"

Drinking Crow

Listening to Sheryl Crow sing a song about Billy
being at the bar at noon on Tuesday seems like a once in
a lifetime event for the sultry, yet innocent, star.

Yet Ms. Crow must realize that words of disillusionment are simple
when chaos streams
along the sidewalk on Main Street daily.

Witness each face walking blindly alone—concerned only with
their next reality fix that will carry them into the next day—or the
next month—or the next year.

Watching the masses washing their cars, then imagining them
going back to work at the record store is never enough.

Too often simplicity carries confusion, common man hides pain…

Too much to witness on Anywhere Lane, USA.
Too much to die for while drinking Bud on a Tuesday afternoon.

Daylight Savings Time

It is still light at 9 o'clock in the evening, isn't it?

It seems that all is well as I look at my cell, seeing the trees
Waving incoherently through the sights of the last rays I focus on.
Hope is never eternal when twilight echoes.
Down toward a mission I never seem to finish.

I walk aimlessly around the house, bump into old snapshots that
Have yellowed with time.
Seize a glance of my trusty jug—catching the final daydream
Along the neck of the half-filled flask.
Sitting now, facing the end of a useless day, flowing terror pursing
my lips.

I drink and toast a piece of the world.
My own world.
My lonely world.

Holy Week

Was I all right to scatter the bones of the savior through
 a Naked bowling alley, where youth remain fenced in among old
cronies who flap their protruding guts over their pants, screaming
"War is Hell," then proceed to flutter the ball down the alley,

knocking down two pins.

Was I all right to scatter the bones of the savior in the secret
worship place, between the praying and the dead, where patrons
of good belief fall into a celebration of an afterlife.

Was I all right to scatter the bones of the savior on Easter—when
grandfathers hold their grandsons by the hand and search for
eggs and death in minefields?

Was I all right…WAS I ALL RIGHT…to scatter bones of the
savior on soiled humanity?

Or was I all wrong?

Rancor

I always liked the word rancor.

To me, it always carried a silent power—a fearful alliance with guys who
wore tattoos with pride and spit chewing tobacco on little Joey's
shoes.
Rancor: acrimony, animosity, antagonism, aversion, bitterness.
Words associated with those that curse the daily grind.
Spilling their guts just to exist.

I enjoy a cup of rancor every morning with cream and sugar.
Helps me to hate the day just a little bit more.

The 21st Century Wretch
Scintillating Publications, 2007
Joseph Veronneau, Editor

The 21ˢᵗ Century Wretch

Four days on the bottle and no secrets solved.
Only a better appreciation for the Beatles and Beat poetry.

To stagger among the ruins—newspaper clippings in infected side-
walks, yellowed
With Christmas specials in July…heat bugs in forgotten alleys that
chop away
Tarnished skin.

The stance of a leper, falling out of the dusk—hoping some lost lyric
will help
Find the way.

Barefoot, unkempt, unwanted, and provoked to die in a pool of
drowning sweat.
Cumbersome, tired, and falling…falling…falling.

Out of sight.
Out of mind.

Following the Cigar Store All-Star in Boston

Being able to walk
rank and file amongst
stoic suit and tie heroes,
you must invest 50 dollars
at the nearest cigar store.

Flair your nostrils along the tobacco dick.

Then pull out your personal lighter
and start sucking away.

Puff your chest in pride
as you make huge zeroes with the cigar smoke.

Beam with prestige when you leave the store—knowing
that you have the bankroll to purchase an expensive status symbol.

And, while you walk with your steps of grandeur in trendy shoes,
raising a corporate umbrella, trying to avoid the crimson
red tears that fall from the skies.

Remember.

The city bleeds a little each day
when obviousness becomes
next to godliness.

He Looked Like the Guy on the Aqualung Album Cover

Burnt out from life old man with matchstick legs,
picking through garbage, looking for a piece of
Kentucky Fried Chicken that some Christmas
shopper threw away because he decided he
was too full to finish the 16-piece special.

You witness this and think that you have
some insight on how the bum who survives
poking through the trash feels and reacts to daily events.

The snow spittles around the gay festivities of looking
for the right shoes for Uncle Leo, or the portable DVD
player for little Fred—but the guy with the
Help me sign around his neck is still in view.

Freezing, shivering, looking for a handout to live.
You believe that you have the right to be empathetic about his plight.

Have you ever? (blank).
Have you ever? (blank).

Fill in the blanks accordingly—then continue with your pitiful ignore.

Trying to Pick up a Fat Farm Girl

After I made my smooth move
To get down her pants, she
Said, "I would rather make
Love to a pitchfork."

Looking back—maybe I
Should have changed
My pick-up strategy.

Telling an obese girl that
You would like to go home
And "swap some fat," might
Not be the phrase I should have
Used to help me get laid.

Unless, of course, we were going
to get really kinky.

And make love while bathing in lard.

Wellbutrin Blues

When the will cannot find a way to converse with all the budding
failures of women
who are waiting for the 4 PM bus.

I will retreat into my shell of gazing incoherently.
Blaming the new medication I am on for chronic depression.

Finding mental murder without actually hurting anyone.

Hanna Barbera Vs. Loose Woman

Touché Turtle and
Ricochet Rabbit had no
clue on how to approach
women while concealing a hard-on.
As a 14-year-old male in 1976, your
television mind crossed often between
Loni Anderson's boobs and Quick Draw
McGraw's battle with the enemy.

Magilla Gorilla or Farrah Faucet-Majors?
Wally Gator or locker room panic?

Even Edith Bunker looked good sometimes when she wore
that red suit.

Vonnegut, Harrison Bergeron & the "They"

Vonnegut forgot to tell Harrison Bergeron about the 100-day warranty
on his shit detector.

It sold at the "Let's make everybody equal store," where mutilated limbs,
crushed fingers,
and bad dandruff sold in aisles that are covered in molded peanut brittle.

Last week some guy needed to suppress his stylish singing voice so it
would be equal
with the rest of the tone-deaf lepers.

So, he bought a half-tracheotomy and a seventh toe for 8 bucks.

He now sings raspy and walks like he's constantly avoiding stepping
into a pile of crap.

The chains will come later, once "they" find out he can write also.

Everybody must be same, the "they" say.
Everybody must be the same.

God bless the "they."

Drinking Pretender in Rock-Gut Paradise

Fooling oneself has
become life's favorite
pastime.

"You're not fat."
"Your teeth aren't that green."
"You are beautiful…inside."
Right…and I'm Jesus Christ.

Morbid Fascination

Let the guns be cocked somewhere for once.

Such a pain in the ass having the barrel aimed at me all the time—
while in the
process, a frightened, lost child, is continually being exposed and
emotionally raped.

These days, **riding it out** means that a second has passed by on the
clock and I'm still
walking through the echoes of existence.

Hollers, screams, violent disposal of footsteps.

Wandering alone, down an empty hall…filling up my jigger
of forlorn in an abandoned
seashell I call home.

Never righting the wrongs or wronging the rights of life,
just a preoccupation of a casket,
a weapon, and not much time.

Always not much time…

Dreaming Before Suicide

I am dreaming from the groin,
waiting for a sexual dynamo
to take me into her arms
and destroy me.

I was hoping to jump on
a train to Alaska with the hobos,
pretending I'm Jack Kerouac.

I was wishing Ronnie Van Zant
would come back to life and
ram his words down the pencil-
pushers throat.

I exist second by second, influenced by lyrics and poems
by those who preceded me.

Cherished woman that refused to conform to society's norm.

Eventually, I will fall into a six-foot hole, with
only my words and skeletal smile remaining.

Never to be remembered—only adding to a gruesome landscape.

Ode to the Working Stiff

When it seems I have confronted
the final outcry of creative mankind that
dared to raise its beautiful head and
stare at me—I always end up falling into a rockpile
of jaded mailmen and Nabisco Wheat Thin
grocery clerks.

Not Lennon's Imagine

Imagine the death of man.

One man.
Fighting for his last breath before he succumbs to finality.

Imagine a sight.
The last sight.
Of one in a car-wreck or
a cancer patient, or
someone whose just
had it and holds a gun
to his temple.

Imagine hands.
Not a poet or carpenter's hands.
Only hands that are wanting,
praying,
hoping.
Needing answers but receiving nothing.

We will wait and wait while the clock ticks each moment away.
Every second that cannot be recaptured—each second forgotten while
man is wrapped up in his playground creation.

On Being Religious

"You see the light but refuse to embrace it."
Unnamed priest scolding Dan Provost—1987

So, illumination is nirvana?
Or holocaust?

And, if getting out of the shadow means
witnessing millions upon millions dying—why
would anyone want to break out of the dark, seeking
to be enlightened?

What of the alternative?

Sharing the worship plan with a supreme being?
Chanting a name?
Seeing a face?
A belief in glorious immorality?

On what grounds?
What terms?

The sounds & echoes of the world will fall one
day to the silence of some unknowing judgement.

Will it?
Should it?
How should the end be approached?

Is mankind biological—or spiritual?

Is it enough to be gracious, righteous, and treating
your fellow man with dignity and respect?

Or are Buddha and Jesus, correct?

Sing the songs of clinging faith and rejoice with the
others who have taken the cup—sipping from
the sacrificial wine.

The wine from the vine.
The wine from the thorny vine.

Fighting the Fight

Every day at 4:30 AM.
Biological clocks wake biological sad men who give supreme effort to
go about their business.

A tired stare into oblivion serves as a faint hope in justifying why
they rise so early.

It is a blank stare—a red-eyed glare into nothing but another day,
another room, another
chance at faulty existence.

Yet, these men will see the sun rise, understand that a job has to be
done, then slowly
put their boots on and shuffle off to work.

With unwanted grief in their hearts.
Loneliness in their souls.

They will walk in line, quietly obeying the world.

Alone.

In Massachusetts, Drunk Drivers Sometimes Don't Get Caught

With any luck, I'll
make it all the way to
the end of the highway
with the dignity of a snake,
as I creep off the ramp
to a place I will never
be recognized.

I will justify that the
liquor flowing through
my veins will
add to my concentration
behind the fuzzy wheel.

Music, playing on
the radio, will
make me feel

despondent as I stumble into the driveway.
Surviving another gun
to the head.

Day 236 at the Wildwood

The falling rain
has played havoc
With some 30-cent
kid's new pink hair
cut which, I guess,
has caused him to sink
into a five-dollar depression.

He slowly walks into the
Wildwood Lounge, apparently
very nervous and unsure
of himself.

Nobody here cares—they all have more than some cheap despair to
live with, an
addiction to the bottle is enough to focus on while treading unholy
water.

A teenybopper novella where Junior is upset over some decimated
fashion statement is
not enough to turn the heads of these hardened people.

Hope is an ideal that has been destroyed eons ago by veteran,
grizzled, rigid, patrons—
who continue to write blank checks with faceless stares
into emptiness.

Even the hard downpour falling outside fails to faze them.

And no young rebel who is having a bad hair day will cause them to
acknowledge
anything outside their abode of four walls, a bar, and circa 1968
wooden bar stools.

Fragments of Survival

Yes, we hide.
Behind booze, drugs, thoughts of death.

Compose words that might knife some editor in the gut.

People watch—skid row, wealthy & condensing.

We run, we seek—sometimes successful, sometimes failing.
Falling into loathsome trap mode…finding, searching.

Staring, looking away, then give in to temptation, gazing back at the
masses that find
a way to annoy us.

Ridicule us—until the point
of final discouragement.

We are along; time will tick with every forced entry.

Until existence is no more and the snow, the wind, and the fire…
are the
only elements left for the uniformed to witness.

Let Humanity Enter

We all can look away from the devastation seen on TV.

Drink beer, burp. And complain about the neighbor's garbage on our front yard.

But just once.

Look into the eyes.
The tortured eyes
of children
whose only crime
was being born in
a land ravaged
by war.

Break it down in simplistic terms.

Feel the pain.
Empathize.

This does not concern any political agenda, nor is this a question of right and wrong.

Deserving of something better.
Deserving of a chance.
Deserving a gleam of opportunity.

Please.
For once,
just this once,
Let humanity enter.

What's in a Name

While Judas wandered
Through town looking for a rope
To hang himself after selling out
The Son of God.

I bet he never realized that he also made
The name "Judas" obsolete.

After all, how many new babies
Do you know named Judas?

There's a rock and roll band
Named Judas Priest, but they
Have a bald lead singer.

Nobody in the band is named Judas.

Not even ex-hippie parents—who called
Their child Earth Wind and Moonbeam had the
Guts to name their kid after a famous traitor.

Could you see the next President named Judas Bush?
Or the next NFL star running back named Judas Dillon?

Judas Philbun instead of Regis?
Dr. Judas instead of Dr. Phil?
Judas Poe?
Judas Kerouac?

It's bound to happen, but I envision
a jaded rock star or actor, trying to make
Some cheap tabloid headline, naming
Their kid Judas.

Not to make any political statement, mind you,
Just to get their name back in the limelight.

After all—betrayal is no reason to
Condemn a name.

Right?

One-Line Time Frame

Sex is death.
War is right.
War is wrong.

It seems the years between 1960-1982 were the beginning
of innocence lost.

No more playing ball at the local field, due to the fear of children
being abducted.
One-night stands were concern for a disease that no one can find a
cure for.

Dead presidents.
Dead musicians.
Dead emotions.

A war that politicians play like some perverted parlor game.

Birmingham hated the governor, didn't they Ronnie?
"Boo, Boo, Boo."

Heroes are mass murderers—not Hank Aaron.
Soldiers are baby killers…not fighting for our freedom.

The Velvet Underground turns to the Plasmatics who then turn into
the Drive By Truckers.

Kids screaming in concert halls.
Kids dying on battlefields.

Youngsters leaving their bat and balls at home in the corner.

Fallen Empathy
Covert Press, 2008
Michael Grover, Editor

INTRODUCTION: You walk and see the dazed stares of those who sanity left years ago.

Or did reality leave them yesterday?

I walked the streets of Worcester many times, perhaps too many, and observed.

Sometimes at 4:00 in the morning.
Sometimes, noon on Sunday.
Sometimes, drunk myself.
Sometimes, tears welling for reasons I never understood.

These words are my observations while waiting for buses, seeing the Marginally insane, and those that are losing the battle: the battle of life,
The bottle, drugs, or some touch with the game of existence.

Am I a lonesome saint?
Or a justified sinner?

Living in the City

Eyes never meet.

Some old man at Dunkin Donuts talks to himself about how
he has met the devil—how his master's degree in biology
from Holy Cross will help him defeat evil.

People walking the streets, constantly looking over their shoulder.

Graffiti.
Urine in elevators.
Whores.
Displaced, with signs claiming they will work for food or money.
Sadness.
Violence.

This is not what I negotiated when I separated from my wife and
began living downtown, but I should have known
that everything is not related to pine trees, whiffle ball
games, and waves that rattle the shore.

The ocean, which has shown its unheralded strength during the
few times I have seen it these past few years, is
so far from my journey of death that I cannot appreciate the beauty
of the blue, encompassing water.

So, I continue to walk down broken avenues, avoiding the homeless
who
sleep in the park next to my apartment building.

Hoping not to step on a crack to break my mother's back.
Steering of vomit, broken whiskey bottles, and used condoms.

Staring at the concrete…hoping someday to find my
way back home.

Looking for a Cure

So, I'm sitting on this wet bench, waiting for Bus #21—wondering if
The disillusionment I feel radiates around all the teenagers who are
Playing hooky from Doherty High School. They look at me, but since I'm
A pretty big guy—they pass by silently or stare down at their shoes
–saving
Face from the gods of toughness…another day of hard-adolescent prayers
Answered.

I'm still watching for the bus when a homeless guy slinks up to me,
Asking if I have a dollar twenty for the ride to Franklin Street. I tell
Him, yes, I have the money, but it's for me—thus you get nothing.
The man,
Who is wearing a 2004 Boston Red Sox championship hat—looks at me like I
Have committed a moral sin because I do not give him a dime. He scatters
Away—red ripped sweatpants, tattered white t-shirt and I begin to look
Inside myself and wonder if I'm a whole being, or just
a poor participant
In a passion play of the weary, the poor, and the wanna be Latin Kings who
Seem to have a sneer painted on youthful, destined to die faces.

I think about a song, a sad song by the Drive by Truckers— "God Damn
Lonely Love." Now that I am divorced, and have
no romantic prospects
For the foreseeable future, my heart races with loneliness, even though I am
Surrounded by hundreds of people at a Worcester bus stop.

I'm uncertain about others who may be crying on the inside, but I guess the
Misery that people go through is none of my business.

So, I exist, like a private locksmith with no emotion or care, just another
Day of being—facing the flame with lack of concern for anything.

A forgiven species?
A silent sinner?
A favorite puppet?

Another bum passes me…asking for a quarter.
I reach into my pocket and give it to him.

I walk away, gone but not yet cured.

The bus arrives—I do not get on.

WTAG Reports That a Women is Threatening to Jump off the Smith Street Church Roof

This started as a mistake.
She never wanted to be so observant of her
surroundings that every frown or smile would
lead to examination of being.

A stare, punks gloating over some conquest at
the bus stop, conversations about business, trips to
the market, plans for the weekend.

All blending gibberish that melted into faceless
interstates, offering further worthless stories
about a life in a day.

A diagnosis…
Troubled, agitated, depressed, all DMS III jargon,
giving confused emotions a nice label.

A dysfunctional hero, a woman on the maladjusted brink.

Ends with a jump off the Smith Street Church roof.

Hesse in Worcester

This city is a micro cosmism of a new era of
Steppenwolf's.

Droughts between eons of smirking cell phone
calls to object "bitches," while standing between
buildings that were built in 1890.

Stained erections ignoring or terrorizing the other.

The smells of youthful death and aged life
seep through every zit and wrinkled pore.

Dresses worn too long.
Pants too big.

Loud bass guitars streaming from chrome cars.
Silent Mozart plays in musty elders' homes.

In the middle stands latitudes of social dismemberment.

Observing, always observing…never succumbing to normalcy.

Unfortunately, a True Story

A chained crew of prisoners marched down the road
as Sweet Lucy raced into the bar.

She did not want anyone to see her staring at the men—
But the sight of hot, sweaty guys who were about go back
to live in a twelve-foot cell really got her juices flowing.

Even she couldn't explain why, but as she stared out the
dirty window of the Red Baron Pub.

Watching the convicted parade walk into the prison van,

she began playing with herself—in front of everyone.

All two of us.

Old Jim, a Vietnam Vet, was passed out.
Snoring loudly with twelve empty Budweiser
bottles in front of him.

The other guy was me, disassociated with society for
the moment, staring into the abyss with a Miller Lite
and a shot of Wild Turkey, ready to be consumed.

Soft moans began to echo through the room as Lucy
got more and more excited. Seeing all those
poor bastards file into the Police van.

The bartender, who at first was laughing, suddenly
became annoyed as she was about to climax.

"Hey you, slut girl…SIT DOWN AND SHUT UP.

"Don't you see we have a deep thinker in here?"

She removed her hand from her pants and looked over
to me— "Who, him…I don't even think he likes girls."

Lucy slithered over to the empty stool.
Sat down, and tried her dirty, seductive look—attempting
To get me all hot and bothered.

"Well, what do you say big boy, you want to duck
into the alley and have some fun?"

It reminded me of a Dirty Harry movie, when some
whore puts the moves on Clint Eastwood—he responded
with a line that always made me chuckle.

"Sorry, only with humans."
I took a final sip of beer and headed toward the exit.

As I was leaving, I heard Sweet Lucy screaming, "What did
you say, you son of a bitch…WHAT THE FUCK DID
YOU SAY TO ME!"

I did not answer—hoping to get out of there before
she threw a beer bottle at me.
Which she did, but her aim was as effective as
her girlish charm,
She missed by a mile.

I left, shading my eyes from the 2PM sun, wondering
about what happens to humans when they die, suddenly
the van carrying all the prisoners passed by—on their way
to Walpole State Prison.

I continued my walk…my journey to everywhere, but
Going nowhere…
Today…

Tomorrow…
And probably the day after that too.

Welcome to Worcester Paradise

Those who have not been stained by the sinister side of Worcester
Meet every Sunday morning at the White Hen Pantry for a cup of
Coffee and discussions of outcast warmth & sympathy.

They all live in a hi-rise studio apartment building above the store, a
Place that is also occupied by festive losers, regarded whores, and
Chambermaids to the heroin queen.

Some come alone, others help those who need assistance.
The woman in the wheelchair, the skinny man with the penny-loafers
And square knot tie.

The lady who lost her son in a drunk driving accident—who never
Emotionally recovered.

An older man tells of his anticipation of seeing his son
over the holidays.
"I haven't seen my Joey in ten years, she tells the group—
tears welling
Within tired, stormy eyes.

A heavy-set woman discusses her battle with diabetes, "I've felt pretty
Good this week, not much pain," as she shifts her walker upright
In order to get another doughnut.

The guy with the circa 1940 clothes, who is terrorized daily by the
Thugs who run amuck up and down Main Street, listens intently to
Every story told—not saying a word.

He is accepted here, and for him, that's good enough.

As I walk into the store to buy a paper, I receive stares from all
Of them…
Those who never got a break.

Those who never had peace in their lives.
Those who will probably die soon, victims of unfounded hatred or un-
wanted loneliness.

My own existence has been one of chosen isolation; I have decided to
live this way.

But not these people, they are prisoners of tranquil want, casualties of a
city whose
Young inhabitants have left them fearful of living.

The loners, the frail, the weak; huddled in their one sacred place on an
early Sunday.

I did not return their glances, but looked down at the floor as I received
my change
Making my way to the exit.

I had the desire to cry, but instead, I took the elevator and entered my
abode of death.

Hoping, when it's my turn to kick—they will find me with a scowl on my
face and a
Dagger in my mouth; enough to stifle the eternal scream we all must
echo someday.

To the Homeless Guy on Belmont Street

I'm sorry I didn't buy a Worcester Telegram newspaper from you today.

I'm sure you saw me furiously hide my face as you approached my truck—I
Was surprised and angered with your utter disregard of
my privacy & patience.

But you do remember the one time I tried to remain virginial, I thought the
Lord would look down on me with a smile as I bought a paper, letting you
Keep the change

A whole 50 cents.

I even acknowledge your wife, who sat on the curb with the obligatory
"help us we're homeless" sign hung around her neck.

Like Coleridge's albatross.
Like Coleridge's albatross.

I hope your plight gets better, and you can find some semblance in your life,
at least
A place to live so you can kick up your feet.

But in the meantime, you'll see more like me…
A population filled with little care for you or your sign-bearing wife.

Except when we want some stopgap salvation by showing
Enough motor skill to reach for two bits in our pocket.

Sometimes Incomplete

Severance pay for living is never collected
When the widow lays her husband in the
Garbage along with the rest of the dead love
Letters
That wither with
Time.

No Guardian Insurance man will be sending a check, nor will
A Hearst full of flowers drive down Main Street with lighted
Autos in tow.

It is the alone who die, shriveled inside a
Closet like abode—who will never hear the
Horns of a celebratory band. No, a story
Of failure is still only taken at face value in
An obituary buried on page 37 in the
Worcester Telegram & Gazette.

The young will still ride their scooters the
First warm day of spring, never considering the
Demise…When time will be spent forever
In the dark.

The old will trim the one small hedge in
The yard: wondering why they still have a five year
Old calendar hanging in the broom closet.

Then more will die—some eulogized, some left
To the rats.
Some old, some young, some never loved, others adored.

Some thought of daily, others never mentioned again.

Simplicity at its Finest

As I walked to my truck with the usual
Scowl on my face, a little girl left the grasp
Of her mother's hand to ask me a question.

"Hey mister, are you OK?"

It was then I realized that there was a God.

Another Example of Realism

I look for my name in neon lights.
But it seems to fit better on a police blotter.

With a pocket of emptied visions, unused condoms,
And broken promises.

As I shuffle from my cell and pay my obligatory fine
To the bored bailiff.

I open the jailhouse doors, adjusting my eyes to
The 6:00 AM sun.
Alive, but somewhat defeated.

Near Christmas, 2007

Alone…
With a view of some
Cheap Nirvana in my soul.

I will seek and find nothing.

ZZ Top sang Jesus Just Left Chicago once.

Maybe he'll end up on
Watson Avenue—looking for
Revenge for all the mortal
Sins
I
Committed.

The blinking Christmas lights
Are worn on triple-decker apartments.

Lower world seeking Jesus joy.

I will walk among the restless purgatory engorged imposters
And wait for the Son of God to confront me.

I hope he's in a good mood.

Thoughts While on Bus Route 21

A Puerto Rican woman will wander into the wrong bus, trying
To explain in Spanish where she is trying to go.
A black kid, already late for school will roll his eyes…anxiety
Leading him to shake his work boot laden feet.
A white guy will keep looking at his watch…needing to get to
His executive meeting. No chance for coffee now.
A blind man will stare into oblivion…petting his dog.
A shy girl will look down at her coat…noticing a small rip
Near the fourth button.
People will watch from the outside, not caring about anything
But the cold weather.
The Bus Driver will his patience and tell the Puerto Rican
Lady to catch the next bus that stops at CVS.
Suddenly…the world never stops, and we are directed to
Stage 42.

The little boy is decapitated in Maine.
The 13-year-old girl is gang raped and drowned in some
Small Connecticut town.
The old man is kicked in the head 50 times on Main
Street South.
A young man goes to war.
The protesters will preach about peace at the Worcester
Court House, carrying signs & singing songs.

The bus drives up Pleasant—to scene 89.

Dogs bark.
The homeless ask for change.
A fat woman will lose control of her wheelchair due to the
Gushing wind, screaming for help.
Teen-age tough guys laugh as she skids down Kelly Hill.

I know my fighting days are over, now, I am hindered by all

I witness daily.
Looking at the survivors wandering, bumping into lampposts,
While I travel on public transportation.
Reading about tragic events in the Telegram, then throwing the
Paper in the trash.

This is existence.
I am home.

Glorified Demise

I see him every day at Dunkin Doughnuts.
Scribbling wildly in a torn notebook.
The cover is hanging on by its last ring.
Coffee stains are his notes on the last page.
He is alone.
Always alone.

Sometimes, I see him slowly shuffle to the library.
A huge backpack acting as a demented cross.
Whatever he's carrying, it is very heavy,
Because he must stop every twenty feet to
Adjust his fat.

He swipes the beads of sweat from his brow—then
Continues to jot at a frantic pace.

He has one magazine, an old Professional Wrestling Illustrated.
I saw him one day reading an article about the old tag-team,
The Fabulous Freebirds.
A hundred times he must have read this story.
Maybe a million.

Once, as I was heading to my truck, A crowd of
People heard his snoring, while sleeping in the park.

The noise, so loud that passer byes looked at each other,
Embarrassed
Of his existence.

After all, he's not that old…He must eat & drink well
Because his gut looks like Falstaff's

But he is homeless
And he reads one old Wrestling Magazine.

And he writes about his slow demise towards
Death obsessively.

No wonder it's a strain to carry that backpack.
Writing a life story about sweating, commenting on Ric
Flair's wardrobe, and composing lonely sonnets must take
Up a lot of paper.

July 8'th 2007, 1 PM

The ledge of City Hall blocks the clock that
Tells the time to those wanderers lost and broken.

I wrote these words while waiting for a bus.
Slightly drunk, strangely feeling obedient
To the human race.

They have their path…I should follow.

Time…Another second of observation.

Another second of staring at the beautiful girl
Who waits for her boyfriend across the street.

Isolated—while searching for that scent of gold.
A payoff that never comes.

Weathered Woman
Ink-Stained Dagger Press, 2008
Alex Nielsen, Editor

Weathered Woman

Lost personas while limping with other night walkers.

Alone.
Bargained for.

Senseless and regardless.

Non-caring for the lustful
surroundings they breath in.

Carrying no anchor or in-between futures.
Just present, waiting for death.

A Nice Stroll

A pigeon's coo sounds
Like an indifferent whore
Giving some john a lackluster blowjob.

The sound you notice while you take a walk
In the degraded city.

Going nowhere…

Why a Guy My Age Should Never Watch a Clockwork Orange

She'll walk on dirty water
As you hide your head in the snow,
Wondering what lust will do to a man
With nothing to gain in this stratosphere.

Her sluttish charm will force you
To read the riot act to yourself.
Upheaval, down slope.

The old in-out or out-in.

And while you bang away,
Feeling the naughtiness of what's showing

inside your trendy clothes.

A frightening figment of techno-erotic punishment
Will force you to go limp.

And your kind.
With flabby arms, malcontented libido
Will soon be over the hill…

In a span of 47 seconds.

While peeking at the new milk-drinking,
Crime slobbering anti-heroes.

On the Left

Swank,
Seductive bar-whores,
Basking in drunken glory.

Observing depravity in flight.
Hazed by sullen dankness that
Flows withing their next shot glass.

A faithful scene scattered in the crusty city.

Where accepted mourners stare.

Many Girls

To all the girls I
Never drank off my mind
(with apologies to Jagger) who
Helped contribute to the regurgitated
Chef Boy-Ar-Dee sprayed in various
Taverns across the Commonwealth
Of Massachusetts.

To all the girls who never wanted
My dick inside them—or just refused my
Gruff sense of passion play.

To all those girls who are now fat, hideous,
And brain dead while waiting for their
Nightmare to come home stumbling through
The door—drunk & despondent.

To all those girls.

I'm still here—betting on the winning horse.
Smiling all the way from tough turf to golden grain.

Sweet Godiva Lady & the PlayStation Kid

Sweet Godiva Lady sells her soul to a twelve-year-old boy,
Thinking he's an enlightened rouge that will carry her out
Of the mid 20-age funk—breaking out of the doldrums.

Bringing them both to some sort of fantasy camp.

So the Sweet Godiva Lady seduces the lad, while he realizes
This happens in underground comic books—he never expected
To hear her say…She's in love with him.

A dyslectic romantic story, only whispered about, during recess or
homeroom.

Seductive stare between student & teacher.
A real Nabokov tale.

…accusations from the school board and warrants from the local
police.
Even after jail time, Sweet Godiva Lady's face and the boy's
silhouette are seen on the TV inquiry shows.

They make passionate love after his backpack is
Found with a ham sandwich and a box of trojans.

It will end all right.

Movie deals, book rights, money.

Some partake in this love/lust/statutory rape
The easy way…Others suffer, then proceed.

Psychotic Slut

Fashionably observant but
Morally confused—she loves
The young boys with the passion
Of a cheap goddess.

Her snow,
Small hands, scratching nails down a
Muscular back.
White summer dress, now thrown on the floor.

She will love, then hate—spit and chew until it is
Time for her senses to appear.

Then she will praise this ritual of folly again, with her
Seduction mask matching the crucifix that dangles
Between her breasts.

About a Past

She's sometimes seductive…
Sometimes shaky…

When entering the tunnel of doom.

The booming catcalls from
The jolly old timers
Convince her to maintain
A passionate view on sultry flirting.

A couple of drinks in her
And you may get the response.
-You're looking for-

Assuring herself that beauty
Never leaves,

-It only hibernates from time to time-

The Southside of Agony
New Polish Beat, 2009
AJ Kaufmann, Editor

"There is no greater agony than bearing an untold story inside you."
Maya Angelou

The Southside of Agony

Layla was a song I thought was written for me.
Forget Clapton's obsession with Patty Boyd.

EC had it easy—he retreated to his mansion,
Shot up dope, and watched the paint dry; while I
Roamed dogged streets on the verge of suicide but

Never had the nerve to pull the trigger.

Now, Eric has gotten over his "true love," playing
On TV with Robert Cray, BB King and the rest
Of the blues heroes.
While I sneak into the Red Baron Pub at 1:30 in the morning,
Put a dollar in the jukebox, and play "Why do Fools Fall in Love."

Suicide

The ending is in sight

A crowd of people
Isolated within themselves.

To leap far away, where eternal sleep will
Sadly suffice.
Shattering glass, wood, and blinds when
You jump.

The mob will talk, forever bonded.
Maybe, someday taking their own risk.

The Far Away Face

He was a face from far away,
Bearing witness by watching the flock
Hear his prayers.

The resonated short syllables echoed
In a small boy's ears.

Where the lad sighed,
Blinked his eyes,
Then walked to the edge of the mountain.

But did not leap.

He was a face from far away; long ago, fabled
On grassy roads—traveled paths taken less often.

Mildly amused, bemused…too tired to
Meddle in transparencies, occupied with
The glow of stars and heavens.

He was a face from far away—once so near
With adroit stares that shot through souls.

But power remained inward, until it was
Too late to leave.

To journey so long,
Without taking a single step.
Taking a small child with him,
Not looking back.

Frightened.

Not knowing if yet victorious.

They are not Friends

Colorless memories of
Slapping ass with the
Bony girl who's crack
Addiction led her to peddle
A death that would not even
Leave skeletal remains.

Yesterday, she cried
When you gave her 40
Bucks—a salary of escape
To worlds of nothing, only
Minutes that lived inside
A tin-foil pipe.

Tomorrow, her life story
Might be on the obituary
Page, not a long tale,
But both of you knew
This when your uneasy
Alliance was formed.

However, what happens
Twelve hours from now
Is unimportant.

Today is now…Your search
From companionship involves
A whore with six missing teeth.

Trying to convince herself she's human,
But understanding her Cinderella redemption
Has been accumulatively lost over years
On the street.

One day at a time lives
In recovery books & twelve step programs.

But sometimes, even the day
Ain't worth living.

The Little Notebook

I carry my little notebook to the park,
Jotting simple observations.

Just to prove I can witness.

To guess people
            Wrong.

Making mistakes about him or her is
The most humane even in our psyche.

It brings us down to the level
Of tragic hedonism, twisted,
Puckered out of
Forgotten kisses and stares.

Yes, yes—I carry this little notebook
In my pocket to understand failure.

To accept, but more importantly
To see all the budding traps
An occasional man or woman
May fall into.

Stable territory in my quiet corridor,
While hoping someday to return
To a place where once, my name was known
And my losses are
            Accepted.

The Circle

Where can it be,
She hears laughter in the distance.

Maybe now taking hold of his
Hand will succeed.

Her circumference abode is
Not camouflaged but aware.

Of Mr. Rabbit blanketed through the
Deep snow.

Of the crow who caws for
The one spectacle then inhabits
The circle with her.

A lone worm—dead and frozen.
Hunted for the warmth of the hunter.

He still holds his soul—for that
One chance to place himself within her.

But…
But…

She is on a journey of enlightenment, a redemption
Worthy of Sun Ra and Apollo to verbalize in legend & song.

She will sail with a discovered radiance.
He will pocket his losses and go.

Away from her rings of chancel beauty.
Because no altar of illumination can comfort
The chances that were never there.

85

Born to Look Down at the Ground
Covert Press, 2011
Michael Grover, Editor

A Way of Life

Depression sucks…it's a murderer of many, the pain of existence.
A lasting relationship with the knowledge that death is around the
corner

That unwanted thing you never want to talk about.
The cheap lady in the goth clothes.

Your nightmare at noon
Your insomnia at 4 AM

This is what depression is
Alcoholism, flimsy drug addicts.
Spouse abuse, jobless—homeless

A shot in the heart from 10 deadly demons.
Depression? Yes, I have it.

For too many years, too many days locked up in black and blank.
Slurping through life on a bug infested couch watching Law and Or-
der reruns.

Crying to the shadows of dust—arranging clothes on the floor
Spare change on the table.

Magazines from last year on the desk.

CDs out of jackets.

Lost, forlorn, disgusted, angry.
Looking for one more drink to get past the plunge.

Avoiding mirrors.
Showering in dirty water
Smell, grime…a filthy sink.
Analysis of spoon-fed steps to the mailbox.
Yes, this is fucking depression. A shrill in
the daytime that no one hears

But you.
And only you.

For it's our little secret. All those who walk like prisoners without
the key.
Bombarded with soot from a hole in your stomach.

Silent yet loud…pounding your head until your ears bleed into the
river of ponder.

Too tired to hear or see.

Alone time with yourself is never scripted,
only feared when the phone is the enemy and
the food on the table has gone bad.

Friends with fruit flies that comfort the pain.
Normalcy inside a spit cup. Phlegm is just
an inconvenience you cough up when there is no
answer out the window.

Plagues of ships sail in no harbor--
but inside your mind…pirates cutting your
throat with memories of being beat up by
the grade school bully.

Spitting sunflower seeds in your hair.
And you, supposedly tough guy—do
nothing but cry in the corner.

Where they know…
They know…

Cruise on whiskey highs
Marijuana highs
Light the beam for a while

Until the come down
Leading to a vile of pussy tears and
Dancing in a false pavilion.

Sickness can take the mind

Where the mind usually does not
Want to go.

But we travel there.
Oh yes, we travel there.

Until the sea and the sand and the wind and the trees and
the heartache of missing her touch.

Becomes passé and almost a basic
ritual to feed the crow again.

Man walks by and you don't care.
Fuck why do you care?

Are you a savior in this dream?
Slammed on the cross or crashed in
A building…

My spirit never could fly.

Not while my trash can is full—the men
die daily, they always do.

My actions?
Mean nothing in the sphere of things

Things that matter, then don't
But that's another argument; is this life
a choice of the living or the roll of the dice
by some goop of a being that enjoys
seeing us suffer.

A masochist wizard
            or god?

I don't know.
I never know.

So, I wake up again
contemplate the knife or the pills
or the building in downtown Worcester
that's high enough to jump off

And kill me.

Then choose neither--instead
I shower and put on a suit
of existence

Refuse to listen to music.
Drive toward fake.

Drown in my own tears
Then repeat the process the next day.

Yes, this is depression, my friend or enemy.
A meddle of the mind, a shotgun
to the soul…where my contemporaries
can turn away in agony. Thanking

Their lucky stars

It's not them.

Queen

When she was

      A new goddess.

Laughing at introspective
Pony boys who saw
Gold in chided sunsets.

Screams from the precipice became
Torrents of rain, a mountain would topple,
A man would cry.

She became the power of lust—unabridged, unbridled,
No story to be told or buttons to push.

Only longing stares and murmurs from men.
Beast in idea.
Lads in performance.

Her kind never fades away.
Just takes time to acknowledge the hunger

Feed.
Smile.
Leave.

4:22 AM: Tripping on K-Pins

23 Klonopin and a case of beer;
Still, I talked the doctors into letting
me go home.

Five hours later, I was roaming the streets.
Looking for a new minotaur to battle.

I Am a Bull-God.

Sorry Kid Rock.

You thought of the song—but I
was the inspiration.

Not even trying to kill myself
can stop destination anywhere.

I defied death, went to the abyss…
In my sleeveless shirt.
With no tattoos.
With no Samaritans of mercy to sing to me.

Just an idea…a journey into
Arthur's Season in Hell…

I played sly tricks on madness too Rimbaud.
But refused to say uncle when the
fire got too hot.

Motifs are never simple when the
rain and the wind last seven days
And thirty-two nights.

Staggering for a thought…

Apoplectic lethargy while
tripping through Worcester
via one-way Main Street
(Why do I think such thoughts?)

Knocking on bricks towards eternal love that
pangs when I move the slightest degree to the
left—because I want to be so good in spirt but
the combustible aftershock of a pleasant duration always
leads me back to the mire.

I'm sick of waiting in the muck alone.
Tired of crisis and despair—a wanton creature
of forced defiance.

A slave of misdeeds I thought were true, just a
minute in the sphere of existence.

We are all that (stuck); despite what she thinks, or
he thinks or I think.

Games are for fools who never get to live twice.

Only one chance at the precious.

Never two opportunities
Only one…
One time…
        For clarity.

Tyson & Cobain

Mike Tyson never believed that Cobain could ride on a moon beam.
He was just another brawler, ready to reap the awards of beating
people up.

The intellectual stuff was for the computer geeks and butterfly col-
lectors Tyson must
have thought,

As old Kurt flew to places only a young Rimbaud could fathom.

Mike wanted instant gratification; a wife to hit, a bar patron to
punch–while Kurt craved cerebral…wanting to see the world with
visceral eyes… Brooding about the search.

Blended colors, frightened children….afraid to live in the transient
world of mind-speak.

Tyson now has a tattoo on his face; strained to be remembered as a
great fighter
Cobain is dead… he's buried somewhere in Seattle with a shotgun
hole in his skull.

I wonder if Mikey still thinks of Cobain…and the strange way each
pursued nirvana.

Co-Ed With One Arm

Beautiful girl with one arm walking
across campus. She approaches the
chapel and genuflects.

I wonder if she's thanking the lord for
the day or cursing him because of
the cruel joke he played on her.

She adjusts her sunglasses, does the
sign of the cross and strolls away with
a smile on her face.

Somewhere, someone must be listening…

World Widows

She dreamt of armies,
Men who fought and bled.

Different names,
Different guises.

All tired from strife,
Throughout the centuries of victories
And defeats.

Body counts told to grieving widows,
Whose lovers were sold a bill of goods,
By entrapped loyalty their men
Purged so ravenously into their soul.

The woman cried, present and past.

Roman widows…
English widows…
World widows…

We are born to suffer, not wander
As the famous song once said.

Drifting into slumber…she knows
That one will not come home.

Ever.

Making a House a Home

Kids crying for food as mother wipes
Away the blood from a punch daddy
Delivered after having one too many
At Jimmy's Bar. He is angry after all, no job,
No hope, and for god's sake, no sex for the past three months.

Witness momma sobbing in the corner as daddy
Takes off his belt to lay some more "conditioning"
On his wife of twelve years.
The foundation, built from concrete—shakes as
The children watch their mother being beaten.

This abode is not condemned or even foreclosed.

Just another night on Lockwood Street.

Because it takes more than a hammer and
Nails…to make a house
A home.

On the Wagon…On a Binge
What's in the Bag Press, 2013
Steve Goldberg, Editor

Off the Wagon

Servitude to the liquor.
Cloudy, Friday—1:15 P.M.
Blond hungover bartender.
Another day at the races,
Where to, boy?

The sun is far…far
Away from this place.
In here, we are frozen—in
Deep thought among ourselves.

Did Berryman think this way?

Dead in dim lit shadows, a glitzy
Blackmore solo breaks from the jukebox, scares
Us all into remembering that

We are here for a purpose.
But no purpose exists.

It's Not the Kill…But the Thrill of the Chase.

He was Avant Garde ugly,
waiting for a hiccup in
tonight's potential.

The man wanted a woman.

Old story.

She was a jackknife—
Looking to make a deal
that resembled Robert Johnson's
arrangement with the devil

Her invisible crossbow determined
it would be a 200-dollar night…

To approach, then seize.

The guy has lurid ideas.

The lady, wanted this hunt
to be remembered…

Removing the shiny arrow
from her bra…

peeking over glitter & gold
eyelashes…

Brief salutations—

Do you want a drink?
The timid prey asked the
spider.

"Sure"—sultry, sexy sadist
responds…
Ready to put the trigger finger in motion…

Berryman's Dance of Pain

Berryman's old Henry wanted to know if he was human. Said he has
A few strokes of hair—drank like a fish, but his feet never touched
the ground.

Then Johnny boy jumped off a bridge, couldn't take the fact,
Even though he said it, that life was a bore.

Probably wasn't wearing sandals when he left…Maybe a rayon tie or some
Cheap sport coat—waved to some as he waved goodbye forever…or
Was it just a day he felt cramped?

So cramped that he could not even discuss his problems with Henry.
Just get me out of here—Today!

Even if it means a lifetime.

Of course, Henry is not real.

He's Back

Yea, you know you have
To stop the small steps
Of dying each time you put a
Beer to your lips.

Lushing away the
Thoughts of tomorrow…where
The sadness rolls over and through you,
Like a dark platter piercing your soul.

The nights of your consumption leaves
You to Morrison bets with the mind.

That wet-logged moral less being that
Says fuck you to anyone in your way.

That asshole is still alive…back
In some shit hole dive, smelling like
Piss and drunken vinegar.

Another loser has come home.

For No One
(I Know, the title was an old Beatle song)

Nothing wrong with drawing a little blood here and there.

What the hell, so many never have the guts to—live.

Spending eternity in a smiley fortress, hiding under
Umbrella tanks when the weather gets bad.

Daring no choice but to laugh at bad jokes…

Fake is so fulfilling for some. I rather be
Miserable and have a hold on truth.

See you…Fuck you—I see all of you blend into some Happy Go
Lucky Biography.

Shift away from the sonnets and draw the final breath of someone
never known.

A Dream of Music and City

Such a sad
        Flow of saxophone notes.

Dreams; a city at dawn.
Without hope or clamor for
Wanted walks of treasure.

The music blows but has
No remembrance, just
A prayer…with one wish
That fades towards the sun,

The sun—of life's fever.

When the Walls Won't Crumble

That sad smile helps when
The suicide voices call your name.

Like an old acquaintance you
Really do not want to see today.

But, have no choice.

A Short Biopic Script

Slow and sad acoustic guitar chords.
Footsteps of introspective walks.
Unfocused snapshots of being invalid
While sitting at a bar with other poets.

Face brazen with pain.
Fighting a lone tear.

Too reflective for my own good.

Wear Brighter Colors
Analog Submission Press, 2018
Mark Bruseke, Editor
For Patrick Singleton

Devout

At length
we are born to wonder…
My God is better
than yours—but,
in the end…the same place
will be dark…
Rancid…
Smelling of sweat.

Deep—we will think
for years, but settle
nothing…in failure
mode of whatever
sin may be in vogue
today…

Hey Joe (Sorry Billy Roberts)

If you possess something for a long time, you tend to wear it down —
Michael Hofmann

A dream of
pandered narrative
slices through Joe's
brain as he tightens
his silk tie—follows
his mom to work
and pleases all the
Cambridge, MA talkers
who whimsically fodder
in any pretense
of
real…
Magically bored, static
conversations that present jaded tales
of "overcoming", "turning
the right way" off the
embankment of defeat…
Mother looks on proudly
as Joe bullshits his way
through another tale of
innovative winning…

The gathering claps
politely, Joe kisses
his mother on the cheek,
then jumps out the window…

Suicide on Stage

Even the word
brings biased fandom
to the ancients who
committed the act
to please some
unforgiving, selfish
God, who's tally
column seemed
always in the black…

and no amount of
melancholy piano
music played as a segue
to a commercial during
an Anderson Cooper Special Report
will ever reveal what
the last thoughts are
of someone who has
made the choice while
straddling the fork in
the road….

The Freudian theories,
The Plath poems,
The Berryman leap
into dimensions we
do not know…
Cannot be rolled out
as a tidy model…
Those who hold a
knife while eating
dinner, the pressing
pain in the head
of what they want

to do with the weapon…

Fighting…
Fighting…
Fighting…
The urge to cut,
To bleed…

To call it a life…
Never the same in you, her…
Or me.

On stage, the audience
will grieve into
separate compartments
of forced pain and anger…

The participant?
He ain't saying much…
from grave to final grave…

Wear Brighter Colors

The Johnny Cash all black
Crowd... shamed into
being past their prime
linger in the back of
the line...grunge,
and unkempt all stars
passed them in the
90s as the cool kids.
Look blankly into
the souls of other
deranged social
outcast, and they
never wear brighter
colors...
Neon, cluster fuck,
White teeth shined, Late 2000
chirped, orange stained cult
in some sort of multicolored
vixen chasing fantasy...

What the Hell is It Anyway?

"It" exists.
In the darkest …
Where a little dog is murdered.
And tendencies toward a startling
answer—
Never come cheap…
Junkies ride the cable
to a spiral of existence
within a trash bin…
Then die, claiming
addiction has nothing
to do with it…
"It's just one of
those "things" was the last
words of everyone
on the corner…Who
lapse into a trance
into some sort
of non-committal
nothing…

Facebook Blues

He put a picture
of a shot glass on
his facebook page
which dulled me.
After hearing Berryman
recite how boring life
is by quoting old Henry's
questions of arts and literature.
I find myself wandering through
the social-media lore, hoping to
find some inspiration to type
great words of wisdom…but
all I get is sadness, battles
over religion and football
analysis.
Picking at my wart on my middle finger, I feel
abandoned by my friends and
enemies who mention the same shit
daily…this is not negotiable to me
anymore.
I turn off the computer—uninterested
in the lost love of him or the menstrual
cramps of her…
Divided between the social circuit and
the everyday report that those entitled to report….
I must not read anymore.

Driving off the Mountain

None of you bastards put me here…
I did it myself…

Why Part of Me Hates the Old Man

I remember the look on the
old man's face when he went into
a tirade about something that bruised
his pride…An issue about my sister's boyfriend.
So, he pushed her down the stairs and ranted around the
house, shouting that he was going to hurt everybody
that got in his way.
I stood up to him with a chair and he gave a stare
like he was possessed and blasted after me…My sister said
run, but he stopped, stood quietly for a minute, then broke down
and cried…He kept telling me never to
challenge him again because he did not
know what he was capable of doing…
This is why part of me hates his guts…
Always had to be the tough guy, the psychological
warrior…A man who needed to be feared to
live with himself…

After Reading Metamorphosis

I know nobody wants
to wake up facing another
day of insanity…The
trudge to make it to work
on time, beating last month's
commission payouts. Hustling,
bullshitting, breathing finite
air shared by others who
walk the mask of existence…
Never in my wildest dreams
would turning into vermin,
Struggling with six new
legs and engrossed stomach,
Give me the justification of
Not
    Playing
          The
              Game….

Glenna's Poor Patrick

Dizzying thoughts of
murder while concealing
a knife in his pocket.
Not understanding his love
for his mother and step-father is confused
with a strange bloodlust, waiting
to spill out on his own
bathroom floor…
Patrick,
The savagery that lived
in your head was never
intended to betray you.
Remembering you as
a kid, you were a wonderer…

Enjoyed dressing up in my
dad's army clothes, going on
family vacations with JU and
your mom…the turn
became evident as you
aged—visions became
anger…anger became confusion
confusion became isolation…
Staggering the Lynn streets
for a momentary fix on a
dream that could take you out
Of your head…

Patrick,
That fateful day when
the decision was made to
take your pain away…You
appeared on JU and Mom's doorstep…
Knife in tow…fighting the urge to

kill them… You won, wandered away…
Muttering to yourself about going
back—back to the halfway house,
Maybe to converse with others
who have bared witness to the
inner evil that consumed you…

You took a rope, locked yourself
in the bathroom, and ended what many
call a curse…Death is never an
easy subject to discuss when you
are at cocktail party, or a bar, or
in the warmth of a favorite song…

Nobody cares about "them crazy" people
anymore—they just exist in bedroom stares
looking out the window, imagining what is
the source of pain and internal loneliness…

You are missed Patrick…maybe not by
the whole human population, but by a group
of people—that loved you and understood

a fire that raged…
That no one could control…

New to Berlin, New Hampshire

I've seen too much
sadness in my lifetime
So, I cannot just say stop…
I have walked away from the written
word too many times
to call myself a poet…
My dreams are fables
of uselessness, shame
of isolation…wanting
something from nothing.
Looking, seeing a child
coming home from school
with a backdrop of mountains,
Souls jumping from those mountains...
Frightened of walking out
the door…
Observing from afar…
participation in zero…
No whims or desires to act upon…
Just mumbling and internal torment…
Oh yes, oh yes…it is there…there
for no one to see…walking into
walls…that really do not exist.

Hypocrite

Reporting on misery
        is weak…

Almost cliché,

Do not open your problems
To strangers—

Lie awake
    And die slowly…alone…

Rick Lussier on Bus 6

8th grade assholes
who would tease
and throw paste at
Ric Lussier…A poor
Bellingham Farm Boy
who had big ears and
no response for the cool
kids who were unmerciful
to this shy, unassuming boy…

Being the fat kid on the bus,
And finally relieved that
it was not me who was
being ridiculed…I would
laugh along with the monsters.

Screaming "ears" in unison,
As Rick stared ahead…
Crying and waiting for his
exit from all this lunacy…

I have no clue what happened
To Rick, he went to another school
the next year as I continued to
Fight my internal battles,

I wonder if he is worn and weary
from these traumatic losses many
experience from junior high
tortures…

I wonder if he is dead…
Beaten by his own hand,

As he remembered the paste
in his hair, the taunts he continually
heard ...And the inner
deadly emotional ride that
Bus 6 took him on...Day after fucking day...

Poet's Block #237

Where am I supposed to be?
just plain, average…not content
but not stupid…adorned with
some echo of talent…but a reverse life…
Anguish in heart—sympathy in guilt….

A story that just will not come to fruition.
With pangs of anger…I drop now, leave the word
because I have nothing else to say…
Nothing else to feel…
I am nowhere near my destination…
Only habit driven to melt away…seek
in signs to come back,
Back—to absolutely nothing.

I see the apparatus across the
tiny room…and I am fearful
of what it will do to me…

Where do you go when the lost is found…?

Walkers Can Go

I am dehumanized all you strollers.
You keep going your own way.

I can look down the street and
see nothing...
            Like you never existed.

I Was So Much Younger Then

At my funeral
The laughers will be there
all circled around the corpse…
Convincing themselves
that I had cause
To bleed insanity into
the milieu of fake…

I have no clue
if I am an example
to the maladjusted…

Fraud would do I guess…roamer
of a small prison cell that
I walked many measured miles
towards a demise that I
knew was coming

This is a personal statement.
Sanctioned by no-one really.

Only a poor, sad life
Gone with no fanfare…
No kindly observation
of depressed tryst
with villains, heroes and
Fools…

Tell me a Story

Obscure narrator…tell me a story of how the priest would tell
good boys not to touch girls before church; ah, the youth of belief.
Clinging onto a hope that laughter will be so pleasing before you die.

That's the exodus isn't it?
The thoughts before the inevitable…the
Actions before the burial.

Feel me…

As Pete said—Love Reign on me.

Tear, cry

but not for me.

For us—we are all we must cry for.

All your words, your stories,

Writers, poets, liars—

the filler before the bombs drop.

Obscure narrator; bridge the gap for another
day of survival…Scan one street of hope

Tell them, feed them security that
help walk into the mire of the day.

Muck and Mire…It is not pleasant.

The Green Room
Analog Submission Press, 2021
Mark Bruseke, Editor

Special education private **schools** are sometimes called "**Chapter "766" schools**. **Chapter 766** (now **Mass** general law Ch 71B) refers to the **Massachusetts** law that guarantees the rights of children with special needs (age 3-21 years) to an educational program that meets their needs.
--Massachusetts Law

Job Interview

The Principal, a scrawny, sinewy guy showed
me the Green Room at five in the afternoon.

School was out, everybody was home…

Just me and him and I'm sure a lot
of echoes—

Screams from the past.

But he never led on how chaotic the job could
be…

"Oh, it gets rowdy in here once in a
while…" he pointed out.

"For the most part, and a guy your size,
it really won't be too bad."

He mentioned they would "test" me at first…

See how much they could "get away with."

"After you set the expectation of the room and be
consistent with the rules…I think you'll be fine."

I shook my head in agreement…the hours weren't
that bad…

And I needed a job…
So, what the hell…

Didn't even discuss salary, health benefits
or anything.

I was 22 years old for Christ sakes.

I accepted.

What the hell was I thinking?

The Green Room (A Crappy Job)

Ja'Quell was a Crip.
Threatened to cut my balls off…

Those gangsters
kept coming…

Needing to be removed
from class day after day…

Stevie was a Satan-worshipper.
Said he had something for me
next week…

Still, the demons
kept coming…

Fighting in the
isolation room with
some sixteen-year-old.

Who had a no-show
father, a crack head
mother…

Some psychotic
would spit at
me…

Yelling that he would
kill my parents…

But those troubled kept on coming…

Or I would have to get them.
Tipping over desks, having
books, pens, and any
piece of school shrapnel
thrown at me.

Jamie was a tough
homosexual...He would
get mad if someone made
a play for some kid he liked...

And they kept coming...

Having to hold the Isolation room
door shut with my foot while Chi-Chi had
a breakdown.

Would have to restrain him
so he wouldn't
hurt himself...

Or me...

They always kept coming to
the Green Room...Teachers
and staff would run in terror...

But the behavioral challenged kids
always came to the
Green Room...

Eight hours a day...
Until I could leave and
go home...

Drink some beer…
Hit the pipe…
Look out the window…

Sleep for a couple of hours…

Then start the whole
thing over again
the next day…

Gollahan

He walked like he had a crowbar stuck up his ass.

Dr. Joseph Gollahan: Executive Director of the Bradford Day School and Residential Treatment Center. A credit to his kind . . . if your kind associates with assholes.

Administrators at alternative programs always seem to amuse the front-line staff. The suckers who get punched in the face, spit at, threatened by kids who have a right to be pissed at the world. Gollahan would strut around with the latest textbook on treatment of troubled adolescence under his arm — looking the part of exalted leader in a hundred-dollar Sims suit.

I remember once, while I was in the midst of a violent restraint with a kid who just found out his brother was shot; Doctor Gollahan peeked his head into the "rubber room" to see what the commotion was. When the kid saw Gollahan he pleaded:

"Joe," (the kids called him Joe — it helps therapeutically to call me by my first name he once told me.) "I need to go home and be with my family."

While yelling his request at the top of his lungs, some phlegm accidentally flew out of his mouth and hit Big Joe in the face.

Coolly, he removed a handkerchief from his pocket and told the boy, "That's Dr. Gollahan to you, young man", and haughtily left the room.

"Come back you motherfucker!", the child screamed as he continued to kick, scratch, and punch the anger out of himself.

When he finally calmed down, and the crying ended over his brother who lied near death in a Boston hospital, Gollahan was gone, leaving early to coach his ten-year-old son's soccer team, never realizing the sweat and blood I spilled while trying to stop this kid from harming himself or me. Failing to recognize what he had done to a boy who was hurting so much inside that his anguish almost brought me to tears. While Dr. Gollahan was teaching the technique of a corner kick, I left for the day and headed down to Smitty's bar. He had his reality—unfortunately, I had mine.

Send me to hell on earth?

I'm already ahead
of you. Constant
witnessing of pent
up anger…

A young boy was subjected
to having feces thrown at him
while hiding in a closet.

Part of some cult's initiation
process…

How many times did this
kid face terror?

How many times has
he feared?

Little Jimmy would flip out
in class…

Growling, snarling…
throwing erasers, chalk.

Anything he could get his hands on.

Teachers would run to
me for assistance…

"He is ruining my classroom," they
would pant and drool…Begging
me to remove him.

Which I knew was my job…

As I picked up little Jimmy
like an unwanted, wounded
angel.

Carrying him to the Green Room
where he would try to bite, scratch
and kick me like I was a boxing
body bag.

He would soon wear himself out,
understanding that his realities would
not go away by trying to fight me.

Accepting truth, but not knowing
how to phrase his sorrows—he would
begin to cry…
uncontrollable tears in screams…In a cold
isolation room…Where it would be just him and me.

He would try to speak, but only two words
were ever uttered.

"I'm pissed."

"Yeah, Jimmy…I know," would be my response.

I held and rocked him like baby Jesus…let him
weep himself to sleep…

I would let him lie…take a deep breath,
then wait…

Hoping the next episode, the next
confrontation would not be so taxing…

But that was a lie I kept telling myself…

There were no physical or emotional
breaks—

In this world of real villains
who beat and degraded youngsters and
dared to call themselves human beings…

Finish the Paperwork

While all the world was in neutral…
The caskets, mine-shafts, and CEOs,
all dreaming about the serenity of
sundown.

I was still filling out necessary
paperwork describing all the physical
wars I was in today.

Asking what the situation was that
led to my actions, what technique
did I use to subdue the child?

Could I have done anything different?

I answer the final question with an emphatic yes…

I could have stayed home, had some chicken and dumpling
soup, watch the Young and the Restless after a nap, smoke a
big joint…

Take a shot of whiskey.

Then, sleep peacefully—never reliving the
ten restraints I did every night
                in
                my
                dreams.

Speaking of Which

Bad dreams
…losing physical
control of emotionally
disturbed students…

Thinking to myself
that intimidation is
such a poor measuring
stick in contrasting the pain
each adolescence suffered…

Adults saw my job as a
glorified bouncer…

A big man who could restore
sanity with a snap of his fingers.

But subconscious cares
little about how much
you can bench press…

Cares even less when trying
to subdue and control thirty-five
angry, teenage boys.

The faces of these kids,
today, grown men…

Never leave my four to
five hours of struggling
sleep.

They attack many nights,
consumed with hatred and

vengeful power.

Revenge for having to restrain
their rage…

Their urge to hit, to hurt…

I was a pathetic totem poll
With twenty-eight-year-old
muscles.

Waiting for a paycheck
so I could go to Smitty's
bar…

And forget.

Well, vengeance is yours
adult-children of rape, vicious
beatings, mental and sickening
torture.

You inhabit my skin, my psyche,
my trips to the depths of my mind…

I am forever haunted by your screams.

They will never—
Ever.
Fade away…

Sick Days

It's 4 A.M.
Just fell asleep
three hours ago.

Still drunk.
Still have consumed hatred,
counter transference due to guilt…

You restrained Chad too hard.
Didn't mean too.

But part of you was angry, just
finished a calming talk with another
kid in crisis ten minutes earlier…

Now Fat Chad is calling his
teacher a cunt…

Getting all the other kids involved…

Miss DeLong runs from the room…
Screaming— "I need you Dan right now."

So, I come running in and grab blubber boy.
Slam him to the ground and tell him to
shut his greasy ass up.

Never, never should I have done that…
Never…

Now, alone—rifling through the fridge, squinting my eyes
trying to find a beer or just some deli meat.

Turn to the coffee table and find a joint half smoked.

Problem is can't find a damn lighter.

I look outside…sunlight just over the horizon…
In three hours, you will get in your shitty car,
drive to a shitty place…and face another
day of shitty behaviors…

I count up the sick days in my head…Wonder if
I have any left, then caring less. Get on the phone…

Tell them I've been throwing up all night.

Slam the phone down…sit on my yard sale bought
chair…reach down
and—find the lighter.

Newspaper Interview

The Millyard Daily News, in its efforts to familiarize our readers with educational facilities throughout the area, is interviewing Dan Lounge, the Crisis Counselor at the Bradford School and Residential Treatment Center in Nowhere, Massachusetts. Dan's job is to help kids overcome emotional problems they encounter in the classroom. He has been at the job for eight years.

MYD: Welcome Dan

DL: Thanks

MYD: So, how did you start in this rewarding position

DL: I wouldn't call it rewarding, I was shooting hoops by myself one day when a friend of my brother drove up and asked if I needed a job. I wasn't working at the time, so I said sure. He told me the job entailed working with kids. I said, great—when can I start? He said come in for an interview on Monday.

MYD: Did you have any experience, did you study Psychology, Human Service Work in College?

DL: Na, English was my major.

MYD: Oh, but you must consider helping emotionally disturbed children a worthwhile task.

DL: Why?

MYD: Well, just seeing the face of a youngster that you helped through a difficult time…It must be extremely gratifying.

DL: Why?

MYD: I sense from your short answers that you are kind of disillusioned with the work?

DL: I hate the work. Many days—I'm spit at, have desks and tables thrown at me. Some of these assholes threaten my family, my parents.

MYD: Well, you did know what you were signing up for…correct?

DL: Yeah, I was signing up to be a glorified bouncer at a place where many therapists run for cover when they see me dragging a kid out of a classroom. I signed up for my ankles to become arthritic for having to put my foot in front of an isolation door while some three-hundred-pound piece of lard kicks and kicks and kicks.

MYD: I guess burnout is a reality in your profession.

DL: Burnout? Try evil. What happened to these boys is a travesty. Being the brunt of their anger and brutality is a bad purgatory. Plus, the pay sucks.

MYD: Ok, Dan…I guess that's all we have for today…Any final comments?

DL: Yeah, fuck you and to all those who get into human services in order to save the world…Ain't ever happening.

MYD: Goodbye.

DL: Fuck you

The Park Street Crips

In a moment's notice, five kids
from the same neighborhood got
kicked out of class…

All known gang members, ready
to kick the shit out of the big white boy
who was trying to keep some order.

This was no coincidence, I had to drag one
of their affiliates out of Mrs. Winston's room
two weeks ago…

Embarrassing him in the process.
He was booted from the program hours later
for waving a knife at residential staff. So
I guess, the word was out.

Bradford would pay…

I would be the first.

Shane—the oldest of the crew, was passing
gang signs to Barry…a wanna be tough guy
who was ecstatic playing criminal.

Ray-Ray, better known as Ray Dog to the
student population, has his hoody up, shaking
his head to imaginary music.

The other two, Darnell and Jamieson—just
transferred into the program and were by
no means altar boys.

I told Ray-Ray to take his hoody off, knowing

that my feeble attempt to enforce the rules of the
green room would be met with a pitiless ignore…

No, he flipped me the bird.

Darnell and Jamieson stood up—peering at me…
Barry just chuckled and rolled up his sleeves…

Then, Shane gave the order…

"Posse Up."

Ray-Ray was the biggest of them all, as tall as I was
And at sixteen, already had some big guns.

Darnell and Jamieson were short but stocky…both pushing
Near one hundred and eighty pounds…just out of boys' lockup…

It was clear they spent some time in the weight room.

Barry was a skinny and sloppy fifteen-year-old, but probably had
been in plenty of beefs in his life…

All of them were behind Shane, who began to posture towards me…
They might have been the muscle, but he was calling the shots.

I was about to be in a world of hurt.

Too bad they don't pay overtime for getting beat up.

Chapped

Twenty-minute drive
to my den of filth…

The smell of adolescence
sweat from lying on top
of out-of-control boys who

hated me, the world, the school…

And every fucking thing in between.

Pull into the parking lot, begging
for a shower…take the stained key
out of my pocket to open the lock.

My home is crap…scattered
pizza boxes lying in a statue
of pathetic…two empty beer cans on
the coffee table…weed waiting
to be rolled…

Sink full of frozen food
memories…

I take off my clothes, leave them
in the dirty pile…

Look at myself nude.
Bruised, battered—defeated.

Ready to take the plunge.
Trying to redeem some angelic
pledge…
Some sort of kindness oath I should

have taken years ago…

The rusty water…old pipes
serve as my penance…

Swerves over my body—
Sad and degrading…

I am not proud of my place
in this world…

I am even more embarrassed
that this "job' takes so much
out of me…

A grief mop…anxious to be rinsed.

Morning Glory (A Decent Slumber for Once)

Just on the verge of waking,
you sense a calmness that ruminates
within your soul…

A day devoid of violence…
An hour without anxiety,
a dream of sitting in a cubical
answering phone calls all day.

Your eyes completely open…
Realize it's Thursday.

Then remember…
"Yep, this ride into work today is going to suck."

A Small Café in Somewhere, USA

Thinking of the Edward Hopper
painting of the guy alone in a
diner…

Contemplating something important
while staring into his coffee…

Some early morning hour
in any city, USA.

These dreams are taking place
while I hold Joseph in the corner…

His screaming about a past
atrocity is rhythmic—but a
repeat I heard from Marshall
two hours ago.

I close my eyes and dream,
letting my poetic side take a little
stroll…

Sitting in that coffee shop…wondering
where life will take me next.

Maybe write some famous
memoirs about my pain
and frustration…

About kids being tortured
in so many discarded homes
around the country…

My eyes open—Joseph is

yelling at me to "Let him the fuck go…"

Yea, I ain't going anywhere.

Loretta

An intern caseworker came into
the isolation room while I was
trying to calm a student down…

I was failing…

He was upset about his mother
being arrested again for prostitution…

Not wanting to believe it, he tipped
over a desk and threw a pencil at
a teacher…

Storming into the isolation room…He
demanded to talk to his therapist…

In strode Loretta, a recent graduate of
Cayman College…She was five-foot-four
of great attitude and remarkable savvy for
a newcomer at Bradford.

As she walked in, I looked at her with disdain…
Thinking she'll only add to the problem…
"Mind if I talk to him?"
She politely asked, so I moved
out of her way…

Noticing the striking eyes and calm
demeanor.

As he kept screaming to go home and
see his mom, Loretta stood her ground—

Looked him in the eye and said,

"We can't get anything done until you stop screaming."

He stopped immediately, looking sheepishly at her…
She tapped my arm and asked if they could talk in private.

I said sure and left the rubber room…

Sitting back at my desk, I could hear them calmly talking about
his situation and how to process mother's issues and faults.

She took him back to her office—
An hour later, he was back in class, sadden
but capable of keeping his anger in check.

When the day ended, I saw Loretta coming out
of her office…I thanked her for the help and complimented
her on the job she did…

She looked at me, smiled and said: "That little shit sure
had a pair of lungs on him."

I smiled back, instantly aroused…

I was smitten for six months…

Going out after work with four or five
others…lamenting about our
day and the population we work with.

When, one boozy afternoon—she told me that she was engaged
and was leaving Bradford for a higher paying gig…

Staying for one more beer…I congratulated her for
the new job and upcoming nuptials.

Staggering to my car, I looked through the

empty McDonald's wrappers and Pepsi
bottles to find a cassette.

Layla by Derick and the Dominoes…
I listened to a disheartened Clapton sing
about unrequited love—

Fighting the urge not
to ball my eyes out,
marking another
check in the loser
column…

Sunday at the Beach

So, I was sitting on
a pure/tyrannical
swing.

On Flynn's beach.

On the shitty Sunday before
my reprieve from the house
of horrors

was about to end.

February vacation is just a tease.

The beginning of the week is filled
with anticipation, plans to see the
sights—
Go to that museum or art gallery
you always wanted to visit, but were
too tired from chasing Nick around the
building.

Or you had twenty-three restraints the afternoon you
were planning to go.

Just wanted to get home,
get baked and watch Law and Order reruns.

But that first day of vacation was going to
be different this year…charting out escapades and
planning road trips to refresh…

Not responsible for dragging kids out
of classrooms…

Being spit at.
Being the target of hatred…

No, a whole week of calling the shots
of what you could do…without
any influence from the perverted
peanut gallery.

The first day of temporary freedom rolls around…
You wake up at noon, rested—ready to do
what you want…look out the window…

See the same old shit…

The same old movement of people going
back and forth…

You've become so maudlin.
So dark in your outlook
that you don't give a crap
any more about visiting something
potentially
beautiful…
Like a fucking painting.

Flipping on soiled jeans.
Rolled up on the floor…

Smelling your shirt so you
stink is at a minimum.

Head out wearing cheap sunglasses.
Make your way to the Red Baron Pub…
Greeting the 1 PM boozers whose view of
mankind is a kinship of your own bleak
vision…

Monday—drink for eight hours…stagger home
Tuesday-Wednesday—hungover, stay in bed and watch movies.
Thursday-Saturday—visit parents graves, stop by to see brothers and
sisters…
Go back to the Red Baron and drink some more…

Which leads to today…Sunday afternoon,
shadows from the empty pavilion lead to
desirable thoughts of suicide.

You cradle the beer in your crotch…
Put your hand to your head, trying
to conquer wet
brain from last night.

The waves hit the shore…
They always do that, whether you
are present or not.

One more sip…one last act
of not being the stopgap
loser in a low rent district…

The bottle goes flying as you
get up and
dust yourself
off…

The six-pack is gone…the ride home
is failure…you will be back there
tomorrow.

The ocean won't care.

Facelift

The powers that be
decided to paint the
Green Room brighter
"green."

"The effect of a more agreeable
color will have a profound change
in the children's behaviors…"

Gollahan babbled.

He was pleased with himself that he
contributed to the benefit of the program.
"You'll see Dan, this will make your
job a lot easier."

As Gollahan finished his altruistic
bullshit, Zit-face Dexter wandered
into the new "Green Room".

He looked at me, then looked at the
stuffed shirt beside me.

"Who the fuck is this guy?" he muttered.

Gollahan left the room…
Concerned about dignity… In
an area where the word
…had no meaning.

Following the Moon

Insomnia was a constant
prerequisite with this job.

Maybe others who worked
in this field could distinguish
between professional and private
lives.

Not me.
I was punctured with
guilt and anxiety so often
that my sleeping habits
became
anticipation of horror.

Rolling around in bed, throwing
the covers off hundreds of times.

I became a desperate man—analyzing
every action I took during my eight hours
of private hell
so personally.

These boys…these poor, monstrous
beings—evil behaviors through
no fault of their own…

Captured my hatred of self.

I could not deny it.

Looking outside
through the eyes of
the hideous.

Nothing stirring in this
world made of cheap tin.

Only hatred—for the boys,
for the school, for the staff...

For me.

The Breakdown

Eight years of ____, _____
_____, _____, ______.

Yes, blank.

Churned butter with
a touch of bourbon
to quell the imagined
guns and knives that I
held in my holster.

That last day, I heard a
boy yelling obscenities, a desk
being tipped over—
Some kid begging to
see his therapist…

I looked at the clock…
7:52 A.M. The Bradford School
was open for business.

Closing my eyes, I put
my hands to my face…

I began tearing…

Looking around, seeing that
scrawny principal coming through
the double doors…

Behind the double doors…
I know what's there…

I've lived what's there.

I've felt what's there…

My guts have been torn
seeing what's there.

A bony hand touched my shoulder.
I stared down at my boss,
like I have for so many years.

"Dan, are you OK?" he asked…
Realizing for the first time…
he actually gave a shit
about my wellbeing.

Scanning around the hallway…
Seeing pictures of students who
have left the program so long ago.

I knew them well—felt their hatred.
a thousand times…

Maybe a million.

I whispered to the man I have
had a love/hatred relationship
with for eight years.

Two obvious words at this point…
"I quit."

Taking a deep breath, failing
holding back the tears.

I stormed out…baggy eyes,
swollen ankles, trembling stomach
and all…Retreated to my car…

Drove away…

Pulled over five minutes later
in a McDonalds parking lot…

And cried my god-damned
eyes out.

The Curse
Roaring Junior Press, 2022
Timothy Tarkelly, Editor

Intro: Happened again—needless to mention? Lip Service for
prayers and "good thoughts" until it happens again?
Might not be a next time.

Floyd

They are saddled
     and tired
          marching in another protest.

Faith will never begin
               anew.

Just blood streams the
                 street.

I saw it all on TV.

He didn't.

Progress?

Is it safe to assume
that race relations
really have not progressed
as much
as we like to think?

Or am I talking to
a Klansman, who is
practicing safe distancing…

Smiling under his mask.

Nothing Much has Changed

Listening to Minstrel in
the Gallery by Jethro Tull

while frantically hiding
my face from the television.

Peek through my hands,

See the same scene.

He's dead.

That was five years ago.

After Listening to Van Jones

I am not kind
to anyone
     anymore…

Too many bodies
being stepped over
or necks being
knelt on…

I am a white boy with
a scowl in my
               soul…

and privilege I want
               to vomit…

Seen too much shit to
believe in peace and harmony

all on TV, of course—
never had to look in
the mirror and worry
about
what time I'll be shot
today.

Or be cuffed and thrown
in back of Johnny Law's cruiser
???

Disaster is not around the
corner…It's here now…

My friends are angry…

The bullshit continues…

There will not be
a next time…

This time?

TV With Dad or (Yea, It's Still Around)

The first
thing I remember
seeing on Television

Was Bull Conner
hosing down African-
Americans with

hoses supplied by
his bullshit of
a police force…

To no surprise, my four
year old mind didn't
understand…

Why "those" people
were being punished…

I asked my dad
and he told me…

"Oh" those are
niggers son" …

Turning back to the TV,
I still didn't get why
these kids were being abused.

Years later
have I "gotten it yet?"

I never walked
the path of a
black person…

Obviously, neither did Pop…

Leaving the Pub

Watching the riots
at the bar that just re-opened
after Donny said it was
safe to go back…

I see two guys shaking their
heads—justifying the anguish of carnage to themselves…

"I have a lot of black friends," they mutter…

I drink my beer and leave.

Thinking I'm cooler than any
white man alive.

Knowing I'm not.

Listening to Blind Faith

Can't find my
         way home
seems appropriate.

We've all lost the way,
              our way.
On the verge
         of never
              coming back.

Honest

Throwing this table
across the room would
be the most honest thing
I would ever do.

A real life event.

No comment would be needed.

Silence, sometimes—can be violence.

Wrong

As a young man,

I used to think
race relations
were always perfect
on football fields.

I don't think that
way anymore.

If Orwell Could Only See Mike Pence Now

Winston Smith
loving illegally.

Yeah, I guess that says
it all.

Dreaming from the groin
nowadays—

Will get you shot
by the moral police.

Led by the
human kidney stone.

Who prays in the dark
surrounded by the Pharisees.

& the dirty blond
who never betrays what
she sees.

Tough Time "Getting It"

It's not enough
for white people
to read *Invisible Man*
or *Black Like Me*...

And say they understand--

And sympathize.

Interpretation

Jesus wept
according to the New
Testament.

Obviously, not enough
to carry the new decade
into…

Peace.

 A former collegiate offensive lineman and football coach for 26 years, Dan Provost's poetry has been published both online and in print since 1993. He is the author of 17 books/chapbooks. His latest, *Finding Pessoa* was released in October by Alien Buddha Press. His work has been nominated for The Best of the Net three times and has read his poetry throughout the United States. He lives in Berlin, New Hampshire with his wife Laura, and dog Bella.

MORE ROADSIDE PRESS TITLES:

By Plane, Train or Coincidence
Michele McDannold

Prying
Jack Micheline, Charles Bukowski and Catfish McDaris

Wolf Whistles Behind the Dumpster
Dan Provost

Busking Blues: Recollections of a Chicago Street Musician and Squatter
Westley Heine

Unknowable Things
Kerry Trautman

How to Play House
Heather Dorn

Kiss the Heathens
Ryan Quinn Flanagan

St. James Infirmary
Steven Meloan

Street Corner Spirits
Westley Heine

A Room Above a Convenience Store
William Taylor Jr.

Resurrection Song
George Wallace

MORE ROADSIDE PRESS TITLES:

Nothing and Too Much to Talk About
Nancy Patrice Davenport

Bar Guide for the Seriously Deranged
Alan Catlin

Born on Good Friday
Nathan Graziano

Under Normal Conditions
Karl Koweski

Clown Gravy
Misti Rainwater-Lites

Walking Away
Michael D. Grover